EN SUIVANT LA VÉRITÉ

A History of the Earls of Portsmouth and the Wallop Family

Alison M Deveson

ACKNOWLEDGEMENTS

I would like to thank Lord and Lady Portsmouth for their invaluable support and assistance in the writing of this family history. Thanks are also due to the Hon. Nicholas Wallop and Lady Jane Wallop for contributing their reminiscences of Farleigh House, and to Lady Emma Cordingley for her memories of her father Oliver, Viscount Lymington. I am indebted to Elizabeth Vickers of Elizabeth Vickers Photography for the majority of the illustrations, and I would also like to thank the staff of Hampshire Record Office for making parts of the Wallop archive available for reproduction. The paintings of Hurstbourne Park in 1748 are in the private collection of Lord Braybrooke, on display at Audley End House, Essex. His permission to use them, and the assistance of English Heritage in reproducing them, are gratefully acknowledged. Mr Peter Barker, who discovered Thomas Wallop's seal, generously donated it to Lord and Lady Portsmouth and contributed the identification under the Portable Antiquities Scheme. The photograph of Sir Henry Wallop's memorial in St Patrick's Cathedral, Dublin was taken by Scott Hayes, Cathedral Administrator, and is reproduced with his permission.

Published 2008, Portsmouth Estates.

ISBN 978 0 9558244 0 1

Designed, typeset and printed in the United Kingdom by Hobbs the Printers Ltd, Totton, Hampshire SO40 3WX. Website: www.hobbs.uk.com

COVER IMAGE: *Isaac Newton Wallop 5th Earl of Portsmouth, by Sir Francis Grant*
TITLE PAGE IMAGE: *The arms of the 1st Earl of Portsmouth*

CONTENTS

Prologue   1

The first five hundred years   2

The seventeenth century and the Civil War   9

The family in the eighteenth century   12

The family in the nineteenth century   17

To the present day   22

The Wallop ladies   29

Houses and homes   34

Farleigh House   42

Epilogue   48

References   49

Abbreviations   49

Bibliography   52

Family tree   55

PROLOGUE

It is an early autumn day in 1591. A long procession of carriages and carts makes its way along the narrow Hampshire lanes, astonishing the bystanders with its colour and magnificence. At its head is a red leather coach carrying the impressive figure of Queen Elizabeth. Now in her late fifties, she is still intent on enjoying a progress in the company of her chief ministers. They have spent the previous night at Wield with William Wallop, and are to stay for two nights and a day with his brother Sir Henry Wallop. The Queen has been travelling for six weeks through Surrey, Sussex and Hampshire before arriving at Farleigh Wallop, and has been entertained in great houses along the way in a style to suit her holiday mood. Sir Henry is in his early fifties and has had a long career in public life in Hampshire and in Ireland. He has been in poor health for many years and is spending time at his English home, where he and his wife Katharine are preparing to meet their royal guest. The Wallop family name is already nearly five hundred years old. Sir Henry is conscious of his ancestry, but cannot foresee that his descendants will still be at Farleigh Wallop more than four hundred years later.

LEFT: *A hunting scene at Farleigh in the late-seventeenth century, by Richard Blome. Apart from the costumes, the Elizabethan chase would have looked much like this*

RIGHT: *The tomb of William Wallop (d. 1617) and his wife Margery, in Wield Church. William and Sir Henry were brothers*

THE FIRST FIVE HUNDRED YEARS

The early history of the Wallops was once thoroughly researched by Vernon Watney, a member of the family by marriage.[1] His four volumes are full of genealogical information, and tell us that the family originated, as the name suggests, in the area of the Wallop villages on the border between Hampshire and Wiltshire. Several owners were listed for these estates in the Domesday Survey of 1086, but none is an identifiable ancestor of the family. The name first appears as a surname in the twelfth century, but the earliest family member for whom there are convincing links to the pedigree is a **Mathew de Wallop**. He had land in Hampshire, Dorset and Somerset in the late-twelfth and early-thirteenth centuries and was made warden of Winchester Castle in 1204. Even if this was mainly an honorary post, it entailed duties such as guarding the king's prisoners and maintaining his hawks and hounds at Winchester. Mathew fulfilled it for nearly twenty years.

The succeeding generations are obscure, but we are on firm ground with **Sir Richard Wallop**, who represented Hampshire in Parliament in 1328. From then on, the family descent is securely linked. Apart from land in the Wallops, their main Hampshire landholding appears to have been at Soberton, about ten miles north of Portsmouth. This was the home of Sir Richard's son **Thomas Wallop** (d. 1361). A seal bearing his name has recently been discovered in a field at Nether Wallop, so he must have visited his land there from time to time. He was succeeded by his son **John Wallop** (1353-1438), who held appointments in Hampshire as a collector of taxes and coroner of New Sarum. A contemporary **Richard Wallop**, possibly his brother, was even more active in public life, serving as a Commissioner of the Peace, Member of Parliament and counsel for Winchester College.

John Wallop's son, another **Thomas Wallop**, married Margaret, daughter of Sir Nicholas de Valognes, and heiress of the manors of Farleigh and Cliddesden. Thomas in turn represented the county in Parliament in 1414 and 1419, but died before his father. Consequently the next heir was his son, **John Wallop** (d. 1486). He was the first member of the family to make his home at Farleigh, where there was already a manor house of some antiquity, described as 'a noble large structure' although nothing else is known of it at this period. John Wallop served twice as Sheriff of Hampshire, and also sat in Parliament, but these high offices did not prevent him from being involved in petty disputes with the freeholders of Basingstoke, upon whose land he (or more likely his steward) was said to have encroached. When he died in 1486, the list of his Hampshire estates, which included Farleigh, Hatch, Cliddesden and Soberton, was impressive. He and

The seal of Thomas Wallop (d. 1361), found at Nether Wallop in 2006

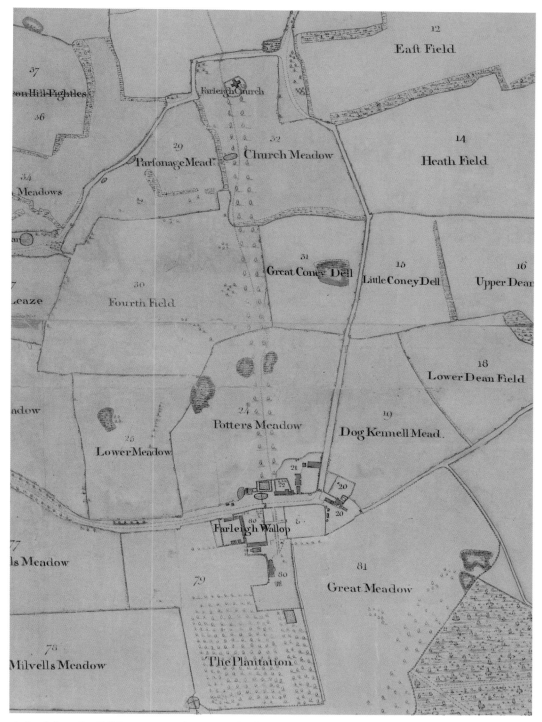

A detail from the 1787 estate map, showing Farleigh House and Farleigh Church

Sir Thomas

There was a Knight at Wallop
In the days of good King Hal;
And he led the men of Wallop
At King and Country's call.
It was Gallop, Gallop, Gallop,
It was fire that none could quench,
When brave Sir Thomas Wallop
Went out to fight the French.

Chorus:
It was Gallop, Gallop, Gallop,
It was fire that none could quench,
When brave Sir Thomas Wallop
Went out to meet the French.

He drove them all before him,
Till they trembled at his name,
On the great day of Agincourt
His sword was like a flame.
"He'll wallop us! He'll wallop us!"
They cried in craven dread,
When good Sir Thomas Wallop
The men of Wallop led …

And when the fight was ended
King Harry grasped his hand,
And "What is meant by walloping"
He said, "I understand;
Your name is Thomas Wallop,
And you wallop till they yield;
So the little Wallop river
Shall be painted on your shield."

Chorus:
It was Gallop, Gallop, Gallop,
It was fire that none could quench,
When brave Sir Thomas Wallop
Went out to meet the French …

Then he went back to Wallop,
And when his wounds were healed
The mazy Wallop river
Was painted on his shield –
It was – Gallop, Gallop, Gallop:
O fast the horses ran,
When Thomas hunted foxes
From here to Abbott's Ann.

Some verses from 'Sir Thomas' by W.J. Ferrar (1936)

his wife were buried in Farleigh church, which from this time onwards was used for family burials whenever practicable.

His son and heir **Richard Wallop** (d. 1503) held appointments similar to those of his father. He had no children, and was succeeded by his brother **Robert Wallop** (d. 1535?), who abandoned a legal career in favour of the family tradition of public office. Between 1509 and 1524 he was Sheriff of Hampshire on three occasions and Bailiff of Basingstoke on four. He also seems to have taken a personal interest in land management, to judge from the references in his will to a new farm and farmhouse, an orchard with a saffron garden and large flocks of sheep. He was outlived by his third wife, who was known as Dame Rose. She was a strong and quarrelsome character, of whom it was once written 'where it has pleased God to call to his mercy Sir Robert Wallop, I wish it had pleased him to have taken that good lady, his wife, to have kept company with her husband to Heaven, and prevented her procuring further trouble'.[2]

In spite of his three marriages, Robert Wallop was childless and, as he had outlived his brothers, the estates descended to his nephew Sir John Wallop (d. 1551). He was the first member of the family to make a lasting name for himself, and combined in his lifetime the rôles of sailor, soldier and diplomat.[3] His career largely coincided with the reign of Henry VIII, and his natural abilities led him to play an active part in the king's foreign policies. His first expedition was to the Low Countries in 1511, where he probably received his knighthood, but he is better known for his youthful naval exploits against French coastal towns between 1512 and 1515, first as commander of a series of ships and then of a squadron.

These successes were recalled many years later by W.J. Ferrar, a rector of Over Wallop.[4] Ferrar transferred the achievements of Sir John to an earlier

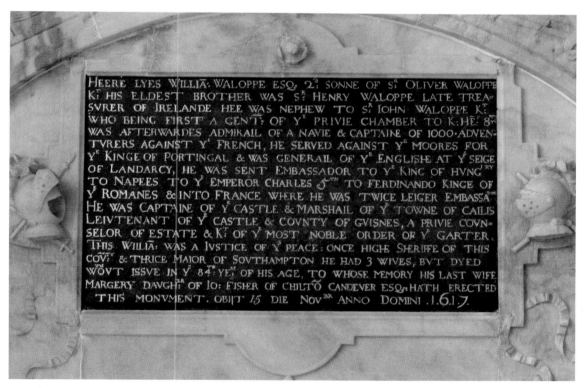

Sir John's career, commemorated on the tomb of his nephew William Wallop

Wallop and an earlier French war, but was right in the general idea of 'walloping the French'. Sir John was particularly effective in a series of raids in Normandy in retaliation for French attacks on the Sussex coast in 1515.

He next travelled to Morocco, where he spent two years fighting for Portugal against Islamic forces. This was followed by three years in Ireland and then a renewed command in France in the early-1520s. The French war was brief and inconclusive but Sir John acquitted himself with distinction. At intervals for the rest of the decade he travelled in Europe on diplomatic missions, and was made lieutenant of Calais in 1530. The castle there was in need of extensive repairs, which he supervised the following year. In 1532 he was sent as ambassador to Paris, and his next ten years were spent largely in France, culminating in the captaincy of the castle of Guînes near Calais in 1540. However, in 1541 he was recalled to England to be examined on

Sir Oliver Wallop (d. 1566)

potentially serious charges of treason. His earlier disapproval of Henry's divorce from Katherine of Aragon had been forgiven but now he came under renewed suspicion of support for the Pope against Henry. It was a trumped-up charge, part of the political infighting which followed the downfall of Thomas Cromwell, the king's chief minister. Sir John gave himself up voluntarily for questioning and the offence was pardoned. Indeed, he was restored to the king's favour to such an extent that he was confirmed in his position at Guînes and elected a Knight of the Garter in 1543.

Renewed conflict with the French kept him busy throughout the 1540s but he did not live long enough to enjoy the peace which was concluded in 1550. He died the following year and, having spent much of his adult life abroad, was suitably buried at Guînes. A confessed Catholic, he had steered a courageous and diplomatic course through the domestic and international politics of Henry's reign and had merited the description 'the magnificent Sir John Wallop', once given him by the King of Poland.[5]

Although Sir John was married twice, he had no children, and his brother **Sir Oliver Wallop** (d. 1566) succeeded to his estates. Sir Oliver fought in the war against the Scots known as the 'rough wooing', an attempt to secure the Scottish border by imposing a marriage between Prince Edward and the infant Mary Queen of Scots, which was naturally resisted. Sir Oliver was knighted for bravery at one of the engagements, at Musselburgh near Edinburgh, in 1547, and was Sheriff of Hampshire in 1558-9.[6]

Sir Oliver's life is relatively undocumented, and we know much more about his son **Sir Henry**

Wallop (d. 1599) the Elizabethan politician.[7] Early in his career he was involved in a disputed parliamentary election, which he lost to the powerful Paulet faction, represented by William Paulet first Marquis of Winchester and his immediate descendants.[8] Although the Paulets were Catholic and the Wallops by this time Protestant, the parties were differentiated by ties of kinship rather than religion, and Sir Henry's cause was not helped by the fact that the election was conducted by a Paulet relative. Knighted by the Queen at Basing in 1569, he finally secured a parliamentary seat in 1572.

Seven years later he accepted, allegedly with reluctance, the first of his appointments in Ireland, where he and his wife Katharine were to spend much of the rest of their lives. Religion and government were, as so often in Ireland, intertwined, particularly after the breach between the English crown and the Papacy. In 1579 the Catholic Earl of Desmond led a rebellion against the Protestant Queen which was suppressed and his lands were confiscated. Sir Henry advocated a scheme for settling English colonists in Ireland, and profited from this himself when he first leased and then was granted the lands of the abbey and castle of Enniscorthy in County Wexford. Here he established a trading community which developed into a flourishing town. He did not always have good health, and several times asked to be relieved of his appointments but permission was not usually granted.

It was during a six-year interlude in England that he entertained the Queen at Farleigh. Family tradition has it that she spent part of the time ratting in the valley called Bedlam Bottom.[9] In view of her age (she had just celebrated her fifty-eighth birthday) it seems more likely that Sir Henry organised a hunt, which she could watch from a vantage-point at the top of the hill. William Burghley, Lord Treasurer, was with her at Farleigh but was too busy writing letters of state to have 'any jot of leisure to hunt or see hunting occupations for a progress'.[10] Unfortunately he did not give any more details, but we know that splendid entertainments were laid on all along the

Enniscorthy Castle, the Irish home of Sir Henry Wallop

royal route, and Sir Henry would not have wanted to be outdone. A few days later the party was at Elvetham, where the Earl of Hertford had transformed his park with an artificial lake and three islands on which to stage a water-pageant and other delights.[11] So many courtiers and servants – perhaps up to five hundred people – accompanied a progress that few houses could accommodate them all, and sometimes, as at Elvetham, temporary buildings or tents were put up. This must have happened at Farleigh too, since although the house was probably bigger than it is today, it was not one of the enormous houses which some of Elizabeth's hosts built for her visits.[12]

Sir Henry was knowledgeable about farming, and was once suspected of having had a vested interest in free trade on account of being himself 'a great corn man'. In Ireland he made a survey of Desmond's confiscated lands, noted the fertility of County Limerick and worked to increase Irish grain production. A few years after the royal visit to Farleigh he returned to his duties in Ireland. He had sometimes been critical of royal policies there, but had earned a reputation as an efficient, conscientious and long-serving official. The conflict in Ireland cost him the life of his second son Oliver, who was shot by rebels in 1598. Sir Henry was finally allowed to retire in 1599, but died in Dublin shortly afterwards and was buried with ceremony in St Patrick's Cathedral although he had requested a simple funeral. His wife Katharine, who must have been equally tired of travelling, only outlived her husband by a few weeks, and was also buried in Dublin. Their three daughters all married in England, and of their three sons, another died on active service in France, leaving only one son, **Sir Henry Wallop** (1568-1642) to succeed.

The coat of arms of Sir Henry Wallop (d. 1599) from his memorial in St Patrick's Cathedral, Dublin

THE SEVENTEENTH CENTURY
AND THE CIVIL WAR

In 1603 Farleigh had another royal visitor – Anne of Denmark, wife of James I. The young Lady Anne Clifford (later Countess of Pembroke) who had helped to entertain her there, described seeing a comet 'which was a thing observed all over England' and must have caused great local excitement.[13] The host on this occasion was the second Sir Henry Wallop. Though he inherited his father's Irish estates, he was more closely involved in English and Hampshire affairs than his father had been, and sat many times as a Member of Parliament.[14] He bought the manor and estate of Hurstbourne Park near Whitchurch, in 1636, probably because it offered better hunting than Farleigh. His was a relatively uneventful life in comparison with that of his son **Sir Robert Wallop** (1601–67).[15]

Sir Robert grew to manhood during the reign of James I. After Oxford, aged only twenty-one, he entered Parliament in 1621, where he had his first taste of the constitutional struggles between king and Parliament which were to dominate his life. James reminded the members forcefully that their privileges were in his gift, and when they protested he dissolved the session. James's disagreements with his parliaments were, however, as nothing compared with those of his son Charles I, and Sir Robert witnessed them all, as member for (at various times) Hampshire, Andover and Whitchurch. When matters finally came to a head in 1641, he signed the document upholding the privileges of Parliament and the Protestant religion and thus threw his weight behind the anti-royalist cause. Though not a Cromwellian by inclination, he was on the parliamentary side throughout the Civil War, and was a commissioner of the court which tried Charles I. He was, however, less than enthusiastic about the proceedings. He attended only two meetings of the commissioners and two days of the week-long trial itself, did not sign the death warrant and afterwards claimed that he had really been acting to try to help the king. Nevertheless he held public appointments during the Commonwealth, and was granted £10,000 out of the confiscated estates of the Marquis of Winchester, his royalist neighbour at Basing, to compensate him

Lady Anne Wriothesley, first wife of Sir Robert Wallop and daughter of the 3rd Earl of Southampton

9

for his losses during the war. These had included his castle of Hopton in Shropshire, which was besieged in 1644 by a royalist force. The defenders were massacred and the castle destroyed. Wallop sold it after the war, along with the rest of his Shropshire estates.[16]

His real troubles began at the Restoration in 1660 when he was expelled from Parliament and arrested for his part in the king's trial. He petitioned, unsuccessfully, for a pardon and was imprisoned in the Tower. There he had to endure the humiliation of being dragged on a sledge to Tyburn with a rope around his neck, on the anniversary of Charles's death sentence. This punishment was intended to happen every year, and he had to undergo it at least twice in spite of his failing health. However, conditions in the Tower may have improved for him after the death of his first wife, Lady Anne Wriothesley, in 1662. The following year he married Mary Lambert, daughter of a parliamentary general, and (presumably following her death) Elizabeth Tompson in 1666. The records of the later marriages once appeared to be lost, but they have now come to light in the register of All Hallows, Barking, the parish where the Tower of London is situated.[17] Elizabeth at least shared his imprisonment until he died in 1667. His estates, which had been confiscated, were restored to the family through the intervention of Thomas Wriothesley, 4th Earl of Southampton, whose sister Anne had been Sir Robert's first wife. His widow Elizabeth was granted an allowance out of the estate rents, but the arrangement was not honoured, and she even had to leave some of her clothes in the Tower in lieu of his unpaid food bills.[18]

Colonel Henry Wallop, son of Sir Robert Wallop

Sir Robert's father, who died during the first year of the Civil War, had shared his republican sympathies. His son **Henry Wallop** (1635-79) certainly did not.[19] A confirmed royalist, he was elected to the first post-Restoration Parliament. Shortly afterwards he was made colonel of a regiment in the Hampshire militia, a title by which he was subsequently known. At some time in the 1660s, during his tenure, Farleigh House burnt down. The fire, which was once thought to have been an act of revenge by Charles II,[20] is more likely to have been an accident, since Colonel Henry was a supporter of the king. The family moved to Hurstbourne Park after the fire at Farleigh, although they continued to use Farleigh Church for burials. Colonel Henry Wallop died in 1679, and his widow Dorothy outlived him by more than twenty years. She was a considerable heiress, and − to judge from the account of expenses - had a splendid funeral at Farleigh.[21] The next three heirs were their sons **Henry** (1657-91) and **John Wallop** (1661-95) and John's son **Bluet Wallop** (1684-1707), named from his grandmother Dorothy's family surname. Henry represented Whitchurch in Parliament on four occasions, and John was Sheriff of Hampshire for a year, but neither was otherwise distinguished, and Bluet died aged only twenty-three.[22]

Dorothy Bluet, wife of Colonel Henry Wallop, by J.M. Wright

One other seventeenth-century Wallop deserves mention. This was **Richard Wallop** (1616-97), a great-grandson of the sixteenth-century Sir Oliver Wallop.[23] He belonged to a branch of the family which had settled at Bugbrooke in Northamptonshire, and he became a barrister during the Civil War. Although an anti-royalist, his career prospered after the Restoration, and he was frequently retained for the defence in state trials during the reigns of Charles II and James II. One of his most famous clients was Richard Baxter, a Puritan theologian who was accused of libelling the Church in 1685 and tried before the infamously bad-tempered Judge Jeffreys. Baxter was fined and imprisoned, and Wallop was severely criticised by the judge on this and other occasions but refused to be intimidated. His flair for publicity had involved him in many high-profile cases, and he was made a Baron of the Exchequer shortly before he died.

THE FAMILY IN THE EIGHTEENTH CENTURY

The early death of Bluet Wallop in 1707 meant that his brother **John Wallop** (1690-1762) succeeded to the family estates while still at Eton. The following year he embarked on the fashionable 'grand tour' of Europe, leaving his widowed mother to look after his younger brother and sister at Hurstbourne Park. After serving as a volunteer under the Duke of Marlborough at the battle of Oudenarde, he travelled to Geneva, where he spent a year completing his education. From there he went to Italy, where, like many other young men of the day, he encountered new ideas in art and architecture.[24] He then lived for a time in Germany and made the useful acquaintance of the Elector of Hanover, the future George I.

Back in England, he first stood for Parliament in 1713 but was not elected until 1715, in the Whig administration led by Sir Robert Walpole. The Whigs split in 1717 and Walpole went into opposition, but Wallop remained loyal to the ruling faction led by Lord Sunderland and James, 1st Earl Stanhope. Their administration fell primarily because of the collapse of the South Sea Company in 1720, and Walpole was restored to power. John Wallop had to give up his position as a Lord of the Treasury, but was compensated by being elevated to the House of Lords as Baron Wallop and **Viscount Lymington**. He is also said to have been made Hereditary Bailiff of Burley in the New Forest, which entitled him to take two stags annually with a bow and arrow, but the origin of his claim to the appointment is obscure.[25]

John Wallop took little part in politics during the next ten years, but re-established his loyalty to Walpole and in the 1730s was rewarded with a string of Hampshire appointments, from Lord Lieutenant to Governor of the Isle of Wight. All of these were terminated when Walpole resigned in 1742, but Wallop was

John Wallop 1st Earl of Portsmouth, by Sir Joshua Reynolds

further compensated by the grant of the **earldom of Portsmouth** in the following year.　He maintained his youthful interest in architecture by remodelling the house at Hurstbourne Park, building another in Marlow and rebuilding the house at Farleigh Wallop, although it is doubtful if he or his family ever occupied the last two.[26]

His eldest son **John Wallop** (1718-49) became

Viscount Lymington in his turn, and began to follow a parliamentary career as member for Andover.　In 1740 he married Catherine Conduitt, great-niece of Sir Isaac Newton, the mathematician and physicist.　Her father Sir John Conduitt had succeeded Newton as Master of the Mint, which was an influential government post. Newton, who never married, made Catherine one

Sir Isaac Newton, by Sir Godfrey Kneller

of his heirs. There is an unkind tradition that the marriage of Lord Lymington and Catherine Conduitt gave Hogarth the idea for his satirical painting *The Marriage Settlement*. In this, the Earl sits with his gouty foot on a stool and his family tree in his hand, while the bride's father holds a marriage contract. The bride herself is engaged in conversation with a lawyer and the groom is admiring his face in a mirror, completely detached from the negotiation. Whatever the origin of this scene, Lord and Lady Lymington's marriage did not follow Hogarth's scandalous sequel to the story. They produced six children in under a decade, but Lord Lymington died in 1749 at the early age of thirty-one, and his wife died the following year shortly after giving birth to their last child. He was buried at Farleigh, she in Westminster Abbey where her father and Newton were also buried.

In consequence of his heir's premature death, John Wallop 1st Earl of Portsmouth was succeeded in 1762 by his eldest grandson. **John Wallop 2nd Earl of Portsmouth** (1742-97) was a young man, recently married to Urania Fellowes, daughter of Coulson Fellowes. The connection with Newton was evidently a source of pride; John Wallop inherited, through his mother, Newton's papers, and 'Isaac' and 'Newton' were used as family names for several generations afterwards. The connection with Coulson Fellowes was also important. He sat in Parliament for Huntingdon for twenty years in the mid-eighteenth century and inherited his father's estate at Eggesford in Devon, in addition to which he purchased that of Ramsey Abbey north of Huntingdon. On his death in 1769 his estates were divided, and Eggesford descended through Urania

The grant of the earldom of Portsmouth by King George II in 1743, with the seal of the Lord Chancellor

to her second son Newton on condition that he used Fellowes as his surname.

The 2nd Earl of Portsmouth lived a more private life than his predecessors. He is chiefly remembered for having built a new house at Hurstbourne Priors at the instigation of his wife, who disliked the low-lying situation of the old house.[27] The great sadness in their life, in addition to the relatively early deaths of three of their eight children, must have been the problems with their eldest son. **John Charles Wallop** (1767–1853) was born with an undiagnosed mental disability which became apparent early in his life. He was sent at the age of five to the small school run by Jane Austen's father at Steventon, but was removed after six months, as his mother felt that his condition was becoming worse. She took him to London for a cure but he failed to make much progress and his behaviour became more eccentric. He was certainly not uneducated, as references in his brother's letters show, but in 1790, when it finally became clear that he would not be capable of running the estates, his parents decided to appoint trustees on his behalf.[28]

Urania Fellowes, wife of the 2nd Earl of Portsmouth

Odiham 1st June 1780.

Dear & Hon.d Sir,

I am persuaded you will readily believe
Me when I assure you, that I feel very great Pleasure
in acquainting you that our Vacation will commence
the 22d Instant, when I promise myself much Happi-
ness at Hurzbourne especially if I have the Comfort
to find all my Friends in good Health, and to give
you and my Mama, Satisfaction by the Attention
I have paid to the several Branches of my Learning
since I last saw you.   My Brothers are both well and
joins with me in Duty to You & my Mama,
        I am Hon.d Sir,
        Your very dutiful Son,
            Newton Wallop.

A letter from Newton Fellowes (later 4th Earl of Portsmouth) to his father. He was not quite eight when he wrote this

THE FAMILY IN THE
NINETEENTH CENTURY

John Charles Wallop became **3rd Earl of Portsmouth** on the death of his father in 1797, and two years later his brothers Newton and Coulson arranged a marriage for him with the Hon. Grace Norton, who was fifteen years his senior, a 'pleasant and agreeable lady, but of an age which did not promise prolific consequences'.[29] They were ensuring that he would not have a legitimate heir, and her reward was to become a countess. After some years she enlisted the help of a medical attendant, and social life at Hurstbourne Park was outwardly normal. On one occasion they gave a ball at which Jane Austen was a guest and, on her own admission, may have drunk a little too much.[30]

John Hanson, the family solicitor and one of the trustees, abused his position disgracefully. He began by occupying Farleigh House, where he installed his family and hosted shooting parties.[31] Seizing his opportunity when Lady Portsmouth died in 1813, he had Lord Portsmouth brought to London, where a marriage was arranged between the confused widower and Hanson's elder daughter Mary Ann. Lord Byron, who knew Hanson as his own family friend and solicitor, was present at the wedding and gave the bride away. Lord Portsmouth's brothers did not hear of the marriage until after the event, and almost immediately began legal proceedings to contest it, initially unsuccessfully. Mary Ann and her family consistently used violence against her husband and though he was physically strong, he seems to have been unable to defend himself. The assaults no doubt made his unstable personality worse. In addition, Mary Ann was openly unfaithful, and produced a child by her lover, William Alder. The

Newton and Coulson Fellowes, brothers of the 3rd Earl of Portsmouth, by Richard Livesay

court case lasted for many years, during which Lord Portsmouth's eccentricities became widely known and were luridly described in the press, until the marriage was finally annulled in 1828. Mary Ann subsequently married Alder, and was last heard of in Canada in 1859. From there she wrote a begging letter which was a strange mixture of flowery and impudent language, claiming that she was 'once the lady of Hurstbourne Park' but now had 'not sufficient to buy my daily bread'.[32]

Lord Portsmouth had a morbid fascination with funerals, and would surely have loved to be a spectator at his own. This did not take place until 1853, by which time his brother **Newton Fellowes Wallop** (1772-1854) was eighty-one and had less than a year in which to enjoy his inheritance as **4th Earl of Portsmouth**. He had, however, succeeded to the Eggesford estate in 1792 and adopted the name of Fellowes in accordance with his uncle's wishes. Eggesford became his family home and his public career was divided between Hampshire and Devon. He sat for Andover in four parliaments between 1802 and 1820, and for

Newton Wallop 4th Earl of Portsmouth, by George Romney

North Devon twice in the 1830s, and also held posts in Devon militias as a young man. Horses and hunting were his passion, and the story is told that

> When he died, the hounds, out of respect for his memory, were stopped from hunting for some days. At their next meet they had an exceptionally great run; and the fox found safety by running to earth in the freshly disturbed family vault at Eggesford. The local suggestion was that his lordship's shade, wishing to give his friends good sport, had temporarily inhabited the body of the fox.[33]

Nine children resulted from his two marriages but only one son, **Isaac Newton Fellowes** (1825-91), survived to become **5th Earl of Portsmouth** in 1854. On his succession he resumed the family name of Wallop. He too was a great huntsman, and was Master of the Eggesford hounds for thirty years in addition to owning a string of racehorses. His marriage to Lady Eveline Herbert, daughter of the 3rd Earl of Carnarvon, brought Hurstbourne Park back into favour as a family home, since it was near her own former home at Highclere Castle. Their eldest son wrote an affectionate memoir of his childhood at Hurstbourne Park, where a 'row of

Isaac Newton Wallop 5th Earl of Portsmouth, by Sir Francis Grant

Lady Eveline Herbert, wife of the 5th Earl of Portsmouth, by Sir Francis Grant

fair-haired children' (eventually twelve in all) sat down to cheerful breakfasts and tasty dinners.[34] Lady Portsmouth was sociable by nature, and enjoyed entertaining, although at least one of her guests did not appreciate her hospitality. Henry James was invited to Eggesford in 1878, and although Lady Portsmouth was 'most kind', he found the visit dull and the house cold.[35] James did not share Lord Portsmouth's enthusiasm for horses, and the quiet family life at Eggesford did not suit him. Another author, Charles Kingsley, came to fish at Hurstbourne, and was offered the use of the Newton archive there to write a new biography of Sir Isaac in preference to a previous one by Sir David Brewster.[36] Lord Portsmouth was reluctant to let the papers leave the house on that occasion, but eventually presented many of them to Cambridge University Library, where they are known today as the Portsmouth Collection. Kingsley's proposed book never appeared.

Lord Portsmouth's political views were Liberal, and as an Irish landlord he was able to assist Gladstone in what the statesman described as 'the gravest of Irish difficulties'.[37] The 4th Earl had introduced on the Enniscorthy estates the Ulster 'tenant right', whereby tenants of leasehold land could, in some circumstances, pass farms to their chosen successors. This custom was continued by his son and given legal standing in the Irish Land Bill of 1870. Gladstone offered Lord Portsmouth first a marquisate and then the Garter, but both offers were courteously declined. Acceptance would have implied that he supported all the government's Irish policies, which was not the case, and in addition, he felt that the honour of the Garter was 'beyond his merits'.

Lord Portsmouth preferred Eggesford to Hurstbourne Park in his later years, and died there in October 1891. Hurstbourne Park had been destroyed by fire in the previous January, but there is no suggestion that his death was hastened by distress about the house, as he had been in failing health for some years.[38] **Newton Wallop** (1856-1917) succeeded as **6th Earl of Portsmouth** and immediately set about rebuilding, with the enthusiastic assistance of his wife Beatrice. They had been living at Hurstbourne Park since their marriage in 1885, and continued to do so when the new house was ready for occupation in 1896.[39]

TO THE PRESENT DAY

Lord Portsmouth shared the Liberal views of his father and sat as Member of Parliament for North Devon until his succession to the title. He remained active in politics in the new century, serving as Under-Secretary for War between 1905 and 1908. His bushy red beard earned him the nickname of 'The Red Earl' and made him the subject of many cartoons. His marriage, though childless, seems to have been very happy, but his widow had eighteen years in which to live alone at Hurstbourne Park after her husband's death in 1917. The twentieth century was, as for so many landed families, a time of change in land ownership. Lord Portsmouth had purchased a sporting estate called Guisachan, near Inverness, in 1905, but sold Eggesford in 1913 and most of the Irish estate shortly afterwards. Lady Portsmouth kept Guisachan and invited many friends there until she was well into old age.[40]

John Fellowes Wallop (1859-1925) had succeeded to the title of **7th Earl of Portsmouth** on his brother's death, but not to the estates, which Lady Portsmouth held for life. He based himself at Morchard Bishop in Devon but, being single, was free to travel widely and spent time as private secretary to the Governor of Tasmania. In later years he devoted himself equally to his garden and to service on Devonshire County Council, and was, in the words of his brother-in-law Vernon Watney, a 'very great gentleman'.[41] He died in 1925, and his heir was his younger brother, **Oliver Henry Wallop** (1861-1943), who thus became **8th Earl of Portsmouth**. He had emigrated to the United States as a young man, in the expectation that he would have to make his own way in the world. He did so very successfully, as a rancher first in Montana and then in the Big Horn Mountains of Wyoming, where many of his colourful exploits and achievements are remembered.[42] He and his American wife shared the hardships and pleasures of the early days of settlement in the Big Horns, and their sons relished the freedom of childhood there. Oliver

Newton Wallop 6th Earl of Portsmouth, by 'Spy'

22

Newton Wallop 6th Earl of Portsmouth, by J.S. Sargent

*Oliver Wallop 8th Earl of Portsmouth, rancher and
senator in Wyoming*

Wallop was a larger-than-life character who fitted
easily into the life of the Wild West – physically
tough, an excellent horseman, a crack shot and a
friend of 'Buffalo Bill' Cody. He also sat for a time
in the Wyoming State Legislature and felt no desire
to return permanently to England. Accordingly, his
elder son, **Gerard Vernon Wallop** (1898-1984),
was uprooted from his idyllic American life and sent
back to England to school, in order to prepare for
his future inheritance of the title and estates.[43]

Perhaps inevitably, the young Gerard's schooldays
at Winchester College and holidays at Hurstbourne
Park were an unwelcome contrast with the freedom
of the American ranch, which he visited only in
alternate years. Relief came, paradoxically, with the
First World War, in which he served first with the
Life Guards and then with the Machine Gun Corps.
After the war he finished his interrupted education
at Balliol College. Then, at the Oxford School of
Agriculture, he began to acquire the expertise which
he was to use throughout his life. He developed an

influential career as a writer and speaker on agriculture, and was ahead of his time in warning of the
dangers of arable monoculture and the indiscrimi-
nate use of chemicals in farming. At the same time
he began to pursue a Conservative political career,
being elected as MP for Basingstoke in 1929, but
resigned in 1934 over policy disagreements. The
deaths of his uncle and father in 1925 and 1943
respectively brought him the titles of **Viscount
Lymington** and **9th Earl of Portsmouth**. In
1920 he had married Mary Lawrence Post, by whom
he had two children, Oliver Kintzing Wallop, born
in 1923, and Lady Camilla Wallop, born in 1925. He
married for a second time in 1936 to Bridget Cory
Crohan, by whom he had three children, Lady
Philippa Wallop, Lady Jane Wallop and the Hon.
Nicholas Wallop, who were born in 1937, 1939 and
1946 respectively.

Gerard Wallop had already begun to put his ideas
into practice on the Farleigh Estate in the early-
1920s, with an extensive programme of investment
in new farm buildings and machinery, particularly
on the dairying side. He also built a considerable

Gerard Wallop 9th Earl of Portsmouth, by I.M. Cohen

The 9th Earl of Portsmouth addressing an agricultural meeting on the Farleigh Estate

number of staff houses and cottages, a shop, a community clubhouse and a piped water distribution system. As a result, the Farleigh Estate became a showpiece, visited by agriculturalists from both home and abroad. In his time as Lord Lymington, he did not have the opportunity to apply his ideas to the majority of the estates which he inherited in 1935, on the death of his aunt Beatrice. The combination of death duties and the economic depression of the 1930s made it necessary for him to rationalise his assets, which he achieved by selling the Guisachan estate, and also the house and park at Hurstbourne Priors. He proceeded to consolidate his work on the Farleigh Estate. He had not liked his aunt's vast Victorian mansion, and commissioned the architect H.S. Goodhart-Rendel to turn Farleigh

House, which had suffered after many years of occupation by tenants, into an attractive and comfortable family home. Farleigh House became the hub of estate life and the focus of many social and cultural events, but there were scarcely three years in which to enjoy it before the outbreak of the Second World War.

Lord Portsmouth's books, particularly *Famine in England* and *Alternative to Death*, published in 1938 and 1943 respectively, sealed his reputation as an expert on organic agriculture. He was as much concerned for the people who worked the land as for the land itself, and was one of an international group of thinkers who promoted traditional agricultural methods and values. This group coalesced into the Kinship in Husbandry, which met intermittently throughout the war and was a forerunner of the Soil Association, founded in 1946. More controversial was his involvement in the 1930s with the English Mistery and its successor the English Array, a right-wing political organization with pro-German sympathies. It has occasionally been suggested that Lord Portsmouth's political views could have made him liable for internment, but there seems to have been no serious danger of that. He undoubtedly had German contacts through his agricultural work, but he threw himself with his customary energy into the British war effort as a captain in the Home Guard and Vice-chairman of the Hampshire War Agricultural Committee. After the war he served for a time as President of the Central Landowners' Association and was a prominent member of the Soil Association and other agricultural bodies. However, he became disillusioned with life in post-war Britain, particularly with some of its bureaucracy. For instance, his short poem 'Lines on the Forestry Commission in Bedlam Bottom' expresses his sadness about the activities of that organisation.

> No yaffle stutters at the ash,
> The great beech stems are lengthmost laid.
> Squirrel and dove can make no nest,
> In boyhood shades we may not rest
> Where charcoal smokes from lop and trash,
> For forest schemes are soundly made
> Since foresters have neater plans…[44]

In 1948 he visited Kenya and bought the first of several estates there, and in 1950, after some heart-searching, decided to move there permanently. He had inherited his father's pioneering character, and felt he needed a new challenge, which the farms on the slopes of Mount Elgon provided. In his adopted land he continued to work for agricultural reform, to serve in the Kenyan Legislative Assembly and to sit on environmental committees, even after his farms were nationalised following independence in 1963. His autobiography *A Knot of Roots* was written in Africa during one of the happiest and most fulfilled periods of his life. Sadly, illness forced his eventual return to England in 1977 and when he died in 1984 he was buried with his ancestors in Farleigh churchyard. He had led a richly varied life, and has

been described as 'a seminal influence' on the early environmental and organic farming movements.[45] His grandson the present Earl of Portsmouth remembers him with affection and admiration as an energetic, enterprising and far-sighted man.

The 9th Earl's elder son, **Oliver Kintzing Wallop, Viscount Lymington**, who was born in 1923 at the Old Manor in Ellisfield, was not destined to inherit the family's English estates. The taxes which had so devastated his father's inheritance resulted in the adoption of a tax-avoidance scheme which effectively cut him out of the succession. After Eton, he was commissioned into the Royal Naval Volunteer Reserve in 1941 and served as a fighter direction officer on an aircraft carrier, but was invalided out with tuberculosis, from which he nearly died and which affected his health for the rest of his life. In 1950 he took up farming with his father in Kenya, where the climate assisted his

Oliver Kintzing Wallop, Viscount Lymington

recovery, but the altitude did not suit him and he did not share his father's interest in agriculture. It was said that his ambition was to become a doctor, but that his father forbade it.

He married impulsively for the first time in 1952 to Maureen Stanley, but this marriage lasted only six months. In Kenya the following year he met his second wife, Ruth Mason (née Sladen), by whom he had three children, Quentin, now 10th Earl of Portsmouth, Lady Lucinda and Lady Emma. They moved first to Spain, then back to Kenya, then to England before a period of six years in Australia. In 1965 the family returned finally to England, where they lived in a number of different houses in Hampshire and Devon. The current Earl recalls that the family never lived in one place for longer than three years. Lord Lymington was again divorced, and remarried in 1973 to his third wife, Julia Kirwan-Taylor, but they were separated at the time of his death from an aneurism in 1984, aged sixty-one.

Charming and cultivated, he is vividly remembered by his friends and his children. However, he was somewhat frustrated by life, and although full of enthusiasms and original ideas, he was too impulsive and impractical to make a success of his many ventures. In his time, these included being a Lloyd's broker, a company director, an architectural student, a school-teacher, a social worker and a would-be commodity trader. A very good self-taught cook, at the time of his death he was experimenting with the small-scale manufacture of hand-made chocolates, a suitably eccentric final foray for this singular man.

Lord Lymington died shortly before his father, and accordingly his son **Quentin Gerard Carew Wallop** became the **10th Earl of Portsmouth**. He was born on 25th July 1954 in Torremolinos, and grew up in Spain, Kenya, Australia and, from the age of eleven, England. His peripatetic childhood and adolescence were reflected in his education at several different establishments, including Farleigh House School, which at the time was accommodated at the family seat. He came into his inheritance at the early age of twenty-one, when he commissioned the building of an ocean-going yacht, *Ocean Mermaid*, and took part in the 1977-8 Whitbread Round the World Race. By now greatly enamoured of life on the ocean wave, he undertook many voyages in *Ocean Mermaid* to far-flung parts of the globe. Her total loss in a dockyard fire in 1998 affected him deeply.

Quentin Wallop 10th Earl of Portsmouth, by Matthew Carr

On land, Lord Portsmouth moved permanently to the Farleigh Estate in 1978, twenty-eight years after the departure of the last incumbent, the 9th Earl. From that time to the present day he has been responsible for a major programme of modernisation, expansion and improvement, including the restoration of the family seat, Farleigh House, to which the family returned in March 1989. He was assisted greatly in these endeavours by the timely sale of 300 acres of building land at Hatch Warren Farm.

His interests are wide-ranging, from hunting and shooting, to travel, food and wine and military history. He feels strongly about access to justice and equality of arms. To that end, he was involved in the funding of parties in two notorious libel cases: Hamilton v Fayed and Aldington v Watts and Tolstoy. He has also supported and continues to support various charities and charitable appeals, most notably NCH Action for Children, the British Red Cross, the Game Conservancy Trust, the ARK and the Army Benevolent Fund. A Liveryman of the Fishmongers' Company, he was elected to the Court of Assistants in 2006. By background and inclination a Tory, he is President of the Basingstoke Conservative Association. In 1981 he married Candia McWilliam, by whom he had two children, Oliver, Viscount Lymington, born in 1981, and Lady Clementine Wallop, born in 1983. He married for a second time in 1990 to Annabel Fergusson, by whom he has a daughter, Lady Rose Wallop, who was born in 1990.

Lord and Lady Portsmouth with Arthur and Bedlam in front of Farleigh House

THE WALLOP LADIES

So far, this account of family history has concentrated on the male line of descent, and referred to the ladies of the family only where their lives or property directly affected their husbands. Some of them had fulsome epitaphs which say little about the real women, but some were interesting characters in their own right and deserve a mention in the story.

Bridget Bennet, first wife of the 1st Earl, was 'influenced by the genuine principles of religion and virtue'. Her legacy to the family is a beautiful volume of recipes and herbal remedies, mainly in her own hand but also continued by her successors. She was in marked contrast to his second wife, **Elizabeth Griffin**, who was said to be 'as stately and proud as Lucifer; no German princess could exceed her'.[46] There is a charming portrait of **Lady Anne Wallop**, one of the 1st Earl's daughters. It shows her as if waiting for inspiration before

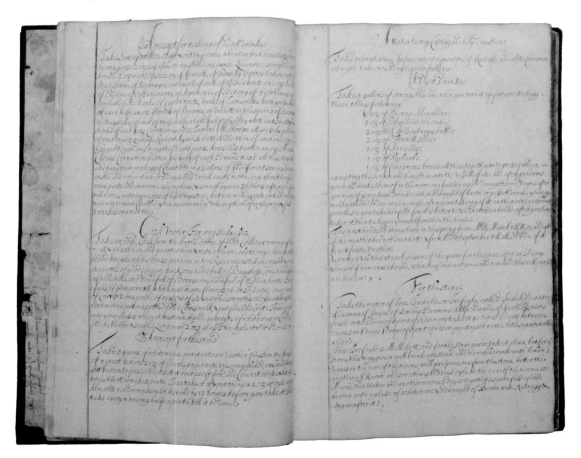

Bridget Bennet's medical and culinary recipe book, eighteenth century

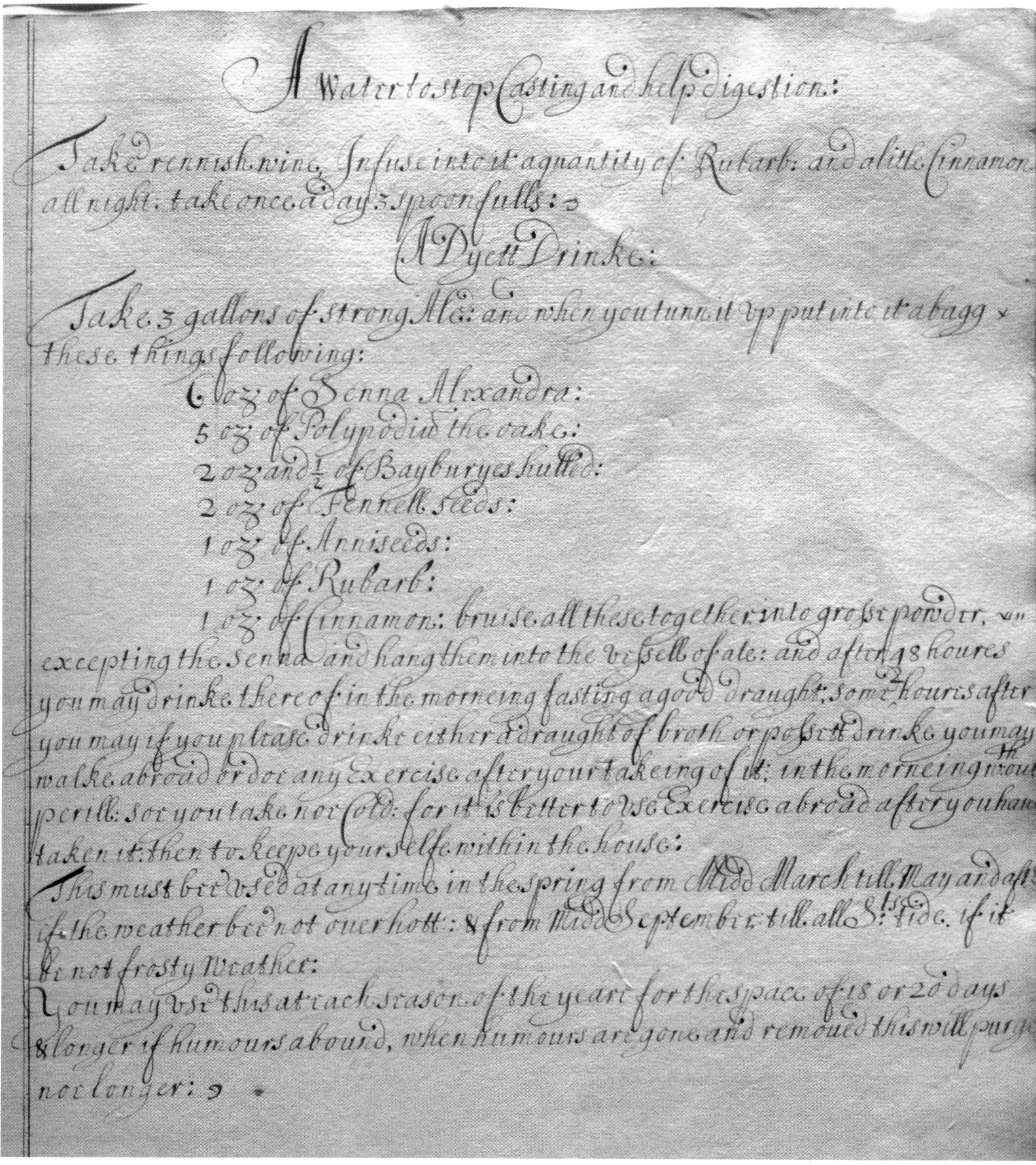

A Water to stop Casting and help digestion:

Take rennish wine, Infuse into it a quantity of Rubarb: and a little Cinnamon all night. take once a day 3 spoonfulls:

A Dyett Drinke:

Take 3 gallons of strong Ale: and when you tunn it up put into it a bagg x these things following:

6 oz: of Senna Alexandra:
5 oz: of Polypodiū the oake:
2 oz: and ½ of Bayburyes hulled:
2 oz: of Fennell seeds:
1 oz: of Anniseeds:
1 oz: of Rubarb:
1 oz: of Cinnamon: bruise all these together into grosse powder, excepting the Senna and hang them into the vessell of ale: and after 48 houres you may drinke thereof in the morneing fasting a good draught: some houres after you may if you please drinke either a draught of broth or possett drinke you may walke abroad or doe any Exercise after your takeing of it: in the morneing without perill: soe you take noe cold: for it is better to use Exercise abroad after you have taken it: then to keepe your selfe within the house:

This must bee used at any time in the spring from Midd March till May and after if the weather bee not over hott: & from Midd September. till allS: tide. if it be not frosty weather:

You may use this at each season of the yeare for the space of 18 or 20 days & longer if humours abound, when humours are gone and remoued this will purge noe longer:

Two recipes from Bridget Bennet's book

hesitation in proposing soon after his first wife's death, and her relatives were surprised but delighted at the match.[50] Lady Catherine and her husband were both very fond of children and had four of their own, to add to the two surviving from his first marriage. As a girl, she had sometimes accompanied her uncle, the 1st Marquis of Buckingham, to the House of Lords, and lip-read his speeches.[51] Her deafness cut her off a little from other members of her family, and she preferred to stay in Devon when her husband took the children to London.[52] She did, however, take a great personal interest in their education, and composed simple dialogues for them based on her own reading, on subjects as varied as the duties of women, and chemistry.[53]

In addition to her many other interests, Lady Catherine was a keen gardener, and created a new terrace garden at Eggesford 'by stealth', collecting a band of workmen

Lady Anne Wallop, daughter of the 1st Earl of Portsmouth, by George Beare

beginning to write – perhaps a letter to the 'young Mr Barton' who addressed her in a romantic poem as 'A blameless soul and spotless beauty joined'.[47] **Urania Fellowes**, wife of the 2nd Earl, left more clues to her personality. Her portrait was described from memory by the 6th Earl as having a 'keen look of intelligence' and an 'indomitable will'.[48] She was the moving spirit behind the new house at Hurstbourne Park in the late-eighteenth century, and was remembered by her descendants for her love of trees and birds.[49]

Lady Catherine Fortescue, the second wife of Newton Fellowes (later the 4th Earl), must also have been a strong character. It was sometimes said that she was both deaf and dumb, but this was not completely true. Although certainly deaf, she had some speech, and could lip-read and use sign language. Newton Fellowes apparently had little

Lady Catherine Fortescue, second wife of the 4th Earl of Portsmouth, by E.U. Eddis

while her husband was out, and dismissing them as soon as she saw his carriage returning.[54] He must have known what was happening but indulged her by pretending not to notice. She also inspired considerable affection in her step-son, and in her difficult brother-in-law the 3rd Earl, who wrote letters to 'my dearest Catherine'.[55]

Lady Eveline Herbert, wife of the 5th Earl, was another remarkable person, 'a lady of rare charm and exceptional physical and moral courage'.[56] As a child she was rather a tomboy, calling herself 'Captain Jack' and leading her little brothers in escapades in Highclere Park. Her physical courage was demonstrated on numerous occasions in later life, for instance in restraining a horse which had run amok and injured a groom, and in helping to rescue men from a shipwreck in Bideford Bay. Her moral courage was exemplified by campaigning in favour of controversial causes such as anti-vivisection and the higher education of women. She was also unafraid to nurse her children, servants and others in need during life-threatening illnesses. [57]

Lady Eveline Herbert, wife of the 5th Earl of Portsmouth, in old age, by Herbert Olivier

She was only twenty when, according to her nurse, 'Lord Portsmouth came to catch a fox, and carried off a lovely young lady'. In childhood, she had expressed a wish for twenty-four children, but had to content herself with twelve. In a diary recording their births she noted stoically that her fifth child's arrival 'made Church impossible'.[58] Her niece, Lady Burghclere, remembered a family life full of tolerance, practical piety, humour, good conversation and hospitality. So many politicians, poets, writers and sportsmen were entertained at Hurstbourne Park and Eggesford that it is hard to see how Henry James could have been dissatisfied with his visit. Thomas Hardy was a guest on several occasions, and indeed wrote part of *The Mayor of Casterbridge* at Eggesford.[59] Lady Portsmouth shared her husband's love of riding and driving, and managed to maintain her intellectual interests in spite of her busy domestic and social life.

It is clear from the tone of their correspondence that she enjoyed a close friendship with her daughter-in-law **Beatrice Pease**, who married the 6th Earl in 1891. The new Lady Portsmouth was a prolific diarist and letter-writer, and took upon herself the role of family historian, making as many notes and annotating as many photographs as she could. She brought into the family a library of rare books and incunabula. Some of the family archives were lost in the fire which destroyed Hurstbourne Park, but much was saved, and preserved through her particular interest. She entertained as wide a circle of politicians, diplomats and artists as her mother-in-law had done, and the warmth of her personality shines through her correspondence and diaries. She worked hard for local causes such as the Red Cross, and took a keen interest in the welfare of the estate workers and their children. She may have been compensating for her own lack of children, but there is no sense of regret about this in her surviving papers. Likewise there is no self-pity in the way she contemplated the ruin of her home and, with her husband, set about rebuilding it.

The 6th Earl and Countess of Portsmouth at Hurstbourne Park

HOUSES AND HOMES

The house at **Hurstbourne Park** which burnt down in 1891 was the first on its particular site but not the first in the park. The estate centre at Hurstbourne Priors originated as a bailiff's residence and farm owned by St. Swithun's Priory in Winchester. After the dissolution of the Priory, the estate was purchased by a series of gentlemen, and then by the second Sir Henry Wallop in 1636. By the middle of the eighteenth century, the residence had been transformed from a modest manor house into a mansion fit for the 1st Earl of Portsmouth.[60] This house stood immediately south of Hurstbourne Priors church, beside the little Bourne river which had been adapted to provide various features of the type of formal garden fashionable in the early-eighteenth century - a rectangular canal, a grotto and a small waterfall. The park, which the Prior had originally enclosed for deer-hunting, had been transformed into a formal wooded landscape with eight avenues converging on a statue, also in typical early-eighteenth-century style. By the time of the succession of the 2nd Earl in 1762, the house, garden and park were all becoming outmoded and the situation of the house was completely at odds with the contemporary idea of an aristocratic residence.

In the late-1770s, the Earl commissioned a new house from James Wyatt, a member of the prolific family of architects and associated craftsmen. The foundation was laid in 1778, and it must have been finished by 1783, because a picture of it was included in a book of engravings in that year.[61] It was a mansion in the classical style, with a central section connected by curving colonnades to winged pavilions. The main rooms were decorated with a great deal of gold, crimson and marble, and were soon attracting sight-seers.[62]

James Wyatt was an interior designer as well as an architect, and was no doubt responsible for the

splendour of the Earl's new rooms. But he was noted for inefficiency in business, and for quickly losing interest in projects after his initial enthusiasm. In addition, his practice was so large that he could not hope to oversee everything, and often delegated the building work to others. In the case of Hurstbourne Park, this was unfortunate. The house was built under the supervision of John Meadows, who worked as an architect on his own account, and does not seem to have been particularly competent as a builder.[63] A century later, Beatrice, wife of the 6th Earl, ascribed the fire to 'bad building, since the flues were in many places only half a brick thick, and insufficiently mortared, and we learned afterwards that it must have been in imminent danger for at least 60 years'.[64]

A plan of the estate in 1817 shows that the Wyatt house was sited in accordance with the landscape style of 'Capability' Brown and his followers - secluded within a park, surrounded by open grass and clumps of trees, and with a view of a serpentine lake in the middle distance.[65] The lake, which has now disappeared, was created by widening the Bourne river with a dam. The garden had a range of glasshouses three hundred feet long, and water was supplied to the house from the river by a 'curious piece of machinery', an arrangement which was ultimately to prove inadequate. A Chinese bridge and various ornamental buildings completed the scene. The new house stood high up within the park, and was approached by carriage drives winding from two new lodges at opposite ends of the estate. This arrangement permitted a lengthy traverse of the park, crossing the stream north of Hurstbourne Priors church and village, and ensuring both privacy and grandeur. A photograph taken after the fire in the late-nineteenth century shows that, unlike many neo-classical mansions of the period, the exterior of

RIGHT: *Hurstbourne Park in 1748, by John Griffier the younger*
© *English Heritage Photo Library*

Hurstbourne Park in 1783, by Conrad Metz

James Wyatt's house had not been altered in any way, and the parkland turf still flowed up to the south front as it had done in the late-eighteenth century, without intervening flower beds or terraces to soften the rather stark appearance of the house.[66]

All the splendour of Hurstbourne Park came to an abrupt end on the night of January 1, 1891. Lord Lymington was living there at the time, but he and his wife had gone to spend Christmas and New Year at Eggesford, and the central part of the house was shut up. However, the furnaces were kept stoked, and the flues began to overheat. Fire ran along the battens between the walls, and broke out in the upper storeys, in several places at once.[67] The house was well alight by the time that the smell of smoke penetrated the servants' wing and the alarm was raised. Whitchurch had a volunteer fire brigade which arrived quickly. The Basingstoke brigade put their engine on the train, and also arrived in reasonable time, but the Andover brigade was detained by lack of horses, which were all engaged for New Year partygoers, and did not appear till three in the morning. The house would probably have burned down in any case, since its construction was defective, the fire was very fierce and there was not enough water available with which to fight it.

Hurstbourne Park after the fire

Hurstbourne Park in 1895

Lord Lymington shortly became the 6th Earl and set about building a new house as impressive as its predecessor. Its Jacobean style and some of the rooms might have seemed anachronistic at the end of the nineteenth century, but indicated the new Earl's desire to live in the manner of his ancestors. In particular, central corridors on the ground and first floors served as long galleries to display paintings and antique furniture, and the great entrance hall had a minstrels' gallery. The main reception rooms looked southwards over the park, and Lady Portsmouth had a private wing built on the curved foundations of the old west colonnade. A large block on the north side contained the domestic offices, and the elegant stables belonging to the Wyatt house were retained. The house was built, as far as was practicable, on the site of the ruin, and used as much salvaged material as possible.

The architects were the London partnership of Beeston and Burmester, but Lord Portsmouth was closely involved in the details, and employed his own clerk of works and local labour.[68] Some paintings, books and furniture had been salvaged from the fire, and were supplemented by new purchases to furnish the house. Lady Portsmouth moved in ahead of her husband on September 14, 1896, and wrote affectionately to him on that day and the next.

> My heart is very full this first evening in the house that we have built together, and I *must* write to you, though besides the one great event, I have nothing to tell … I slept fairly in the little bed in your dressing room, and the joy of once more looking out over the Plain while dressing was very great. I am very glad to be living here at last.[69]

The only drawback was that the hot water was 'all a rich brown'. A collection of photographs taken when the house was finished gives some idea of its magnificence.[70]

The great hall and minstrels' gallery at Hurstbourne Park. The curved carpet was woven specially for the hall

Enniscorthy Castle in 1895

After Lady Portsmouth's death in 1935, Hurstbourne Park was bought by Ossian Donner, a Finnish diplomat who had settled permanently in Britain after retirement. His son Patrick became friendly with Lord Lymington in Parliament, where Lord Lymington sat for Basingstoke and Donner for West Islington. On Lord Lymington's resignation in 1934, Patrick Donner took over the Basingstoke seat, and in 1936 his father gave him Hurstbourne Park. The house had not been altered during Lady Portsmouth's old age, and Donner made some improvements to the domestic block and the servants' accommodation.[71] He also undertook an extensive programme of tree clearance and replanting, which was interrupted only by the Second World War. The house was let to the Bank of England for the duration of the war, and sub-let to the War Office after VE Day. In 1947 there was a

further plan to sub-let to the Ministry of Education, which Donner circumvented by having a bed and other possessions hastily moved back in order to claim occupancy. However, a house as large as Hurstbourne Park was impractical in post-war Britain, and in 1965 Sir Patrick reduced its size by having a considerable part of the main house demolished. The Victorian mansion was completely demolished by a new owner in 2004, and yet another house has replaced it.

Enniscorthy Castle had an even longer association with the family but could not be considered a home after the death of Sir Henry Wallop in 1599. The Norman castle was already several centuries old when he acquired and repaired it for his own use, but none of his successors seems to have spent time there. By the nineteenth century the castle had fallen into decay although the estate was well

The 6th Earl and Countess of Portsmouth with some of their staff at Guisachan House

managed. Some effort at restoration was made, but when the Irish Society of Antiquaries visited in 1895, it was clearly dilapidated.[72] The 6th Earl sold it in 1914 and it now houses a museum.

By contrast, the **Guisachan** estate near Inverness was in the family for a relatively short period, having been bought by the 6th Earl only in 1905.[73] It came with a handsome Victorian house set against a backdrop of mountains. There Lord and Lady Portsmouth entertained fishing and shooting parties, and enjoyed holidays themselves. Lady Portsmouth was particularly interested in the estate workers and their families, and kept a notebook entitled 'Guisachan folk'.[74] After her husband's death she continued to entertain a wide variety of distinguished people, although the journey there must eventually have been quite taxing for her.[75] It was sold in 1935,

largely stripped of its materials shortly afterwards and is now a ruin.[76]

Eggesford House in Devon was a beloved family home for much of the nineteenth century. When William Fellowes bought the estate in 1718, it had an old house which he rebuilt on a new site.[77] As we have seen, the estate came to the Wallop family through Urania Fellowes, wife of the 2nd Earl. The house was rambling and ornate but very attractive, and it is not hard to see why the 4th and 5th Earls preferred it to the classical austerity of Hurstbourne Park. Its only drawback was that it was cold, according to both Henry James and Beatrice, wife of the 6th Earl. Her father-in-law disliked wood fires and would not have them in the sitting-room because in his childhood the logs had always been green and damp, and the fires had smoked.

Eggesford House

Although Lady Portsmouth's own home was Hurstbourne Park, she enjoyed visiting Eggesford and when the opportunity came, did some gardening there, calling it a 'paradise of bloom'.[78] However, Lord Portsmouth sold the estate in 1913, and the house was demolished not long afterwards.[79] Like Hurstbourne Park, it has now been rebuilt as a modern country house.

The family's earliest home was in **Over Wallop**, but although successive members of the family held land there for many centuries, less is known about the manor house than about any other of their homes.[80] Sir Henry Wallop certainly kept a house there, with a 'great chamber', according to the will which he made in 1599, but Farleigh had been the family's preferred home since the fifteenth century. The wheel came full circle when Eveline, widow of the 5th Earl, retired to Townsend Farm in Over Wallop in her old age.

FARLEIGH HOUSE

Farleigh House has been the family's most enduring home, though not always the most used or loved. Nothing is known of the house inherited by Sir Thomas Wallop in the early-fifteenth century except that it was, unsurprisingly, big and impressive in its day. By the time of Queen Elizabeth's visit in 1591, it had probably been extended or even rebuilt. Little survives of this house, but perhaps enough to allow a few speculations. The main body of the house was only one room deep, and probably overlooked a court-yard and terraced garden to the south-east.[81] It is difficult to say whether this house had projecting wings, as was common with Elizabethan houses, or where the principal entrance was. Elizabeth could have approached Farleigh from Wield equally conveniently from east or west. As has already been suggested, the house was not large enough for her retinue, but was of good quality, to judge by the surviving stone mullions which are incorporated into the present house. We know from Sir Henry Wallop's will that the best bed-chamber had a bed of crimson velvet, and no doubt all the other furnishings were in keeping.[82]

Another survival from the Elizabethan period is a

The eighteenth-century façade of Farleigh House

42

The Elizabethan barn

fine barn, which contains timbers felled in 1575-6 and was probably built shortly afterwards.[83] Sources differ as to the date at which the Elizabethan house burnt down. A plaque in the south-west wall reads 'Conflagrata 1661' but another tradition gives the date of the fire as 1667.[84] Certainly at the time of the 1665 hearth tax assessment, Farleigh House was said to have seventeen hearths, which implies that the house was substantial and habitable.[85] Which-ever date is correct, the fact of the fire is not in dispute. More uncertain is the extent of the damage. Parts of the north-east corner and basement have survived and are preserved in the present house. The stable-block (now offices) also appears to be a survival from the previous house.[86] This is borne out by an inventory taken on the death of Henry Wallop

in 1691.[87] He was living at Hurstbourne Park at the time, but Farleigh House was assessed for probate. It had a porter's house with rooms on two floors, a stable with chambers over it, a dairy and other outhouses. Even the dog-kennel was included, but there is no sign that the main house was occupied. During the period of abandonment, members of the family making their wills identified themselves as 'of Farleigh' and asked to be buried in the church there, but another inventory, that of Dorothy Wallop in 1704, makes it clear that Hurstbourne was her home.[88]

In 1731, again according to the plaque, the house was restored. This was part of a building programme by John Wallop, Viscount Lymington (later the 1st Earl). It has been suggested that he intended it to be

CONFLAGRATA 1001 RESTITUTA 1731

The plaque recording the fire and rebuilding of Farleigh House

a home for his eldest son, or that it was a hunting lodge.[89] It is true that the house was on the small scale suitable for a hunting lodge, but Lord Lymington already had all the hunting he could desire at Hurstbourne Park. His son was only thirteen in 1731, and was not married until 1740, but perhaps his father was looking to the future. Whatever he may have intended, Lord Lymington did not use Farleigh House, which was let to tenants almost from the beginning.[90] The park was maintained and the estate managed, as we can see from two estate plans dated 1745 and 1787.[91] But the family did not return there, preferring Hurstbourne Park and Eggesford House throughout the eighteenth and nineteenth centuries. For a time, the 6th Earl seriously considered selling Farleigh, but eventually decided against it, and the house continued to be let until the 1930s.[92]

When Gerard Wallop, Viscount Lymington (later the 9th Earl) decided to reoccupy Farleigh House, he found it in a bad state. The east front, with its distinctive central octagonal rooms, was relatively unaltered, but the west front had been disfigured with various accretions which spoilt the entrance. All these were stripped away and replaced with new rooms on two floors, virtually doubling the size of the original house and creating a harmonious façade. A Coade stone coat-of-arms was retrieved from one of the Hurstbourne Park entrance lodges and placed proudly on top of the tower over the porch. Lord Lymington's architect H.S. Goodhart-Rendel was at the height of his career at the time, becoming President of the RIBA in 1937. The work at Farleigh was finished the same year and the family moved in, for the brief time (as it turned out) which remained before the war. They used the house as the architect had designed it, except that the new drawing-room became a ballroom and was not fully furnished, and the room intended for a library became the children's schoolroom. The basement room in the octagon was made into a library instead.

According to family members, childhood at Farleigh was 'magical', with freedom to roam on bicycles with friends, helping with the harvest in autumn, and mummers in the ballroom at Christmas, but life was inevitably disrupted by the war.[93] Agricultural students occupied the staff flats in the stable block, various evacuees from London and recuperating officers filled the house. Lord and Lady Portsmouth took refuge for warmth in the library and octagon drawing-room but winters were very cold for everyone. Although the house at Hurstbourne Park had been sold before the war, the

estate there had been retained, and Lord Portsmouth built log cabins by the Bourne where he and his young family enjoyed summer holidays. After he moved to Kenya, Farleigh House was unoccupied for some time, before it was leased in 1954 and became Farleigh House School. The present Earl began his schooldays there, and did not enjoy the experience. The grounds were disfigured by temporary buildings such as laboratories, classrooms, a dining-hall and a gym, and the house was again falling into disrepair, particularly the tower in which oversized water tanks had been installed. When the lease expired in 1983, the school was able to relocate to Redrice, near Andover, and Lord Portsmouth regained possession. It gave him great satisfaction to undertake yet another refurbishment of the house, nearly fifty years after his grandfather's and over 250 years after the 1st Earl's. The work on this occasion

Farleigh House in 1937

Robert Fergusson, Lady Portsmouth's brother, receiving a Farleigh House School prize

took over six years to complete, and Farleigh House is now in good condition for the foreseeable future.

In general, taste in garden and park design has varied nearly as much as that in houses. However, the park at Farleigh has been less affected by change than other parks because of the long periods in which its owner was effectively absent. It is a long-established feature, appearing in outline on the earliest county maps and in detail on the two eighteenth-century estate maps. The house and home farm form a close unit at the centre of the estate, with the church at some distance. There may once have been a settlement, represented by 'humps and bumps', in the field around the church, but for many years the church has been isolated, approached from the house by an avenue of trees which have since disappeared. It serves as a memorial chapel for the Wallop family, and was rebuilt along with the house in the 1730s by John Wallop, Viscount Lymington (later the 1st Earl). Remodelled again in the late-nineteenth century, it is opened for

occasional services and special events. The park has always been part of a working estate, used for agriculture, hunting and shooting, and has escaped the more extreme fashions in landscape design. Naturally there have always been gardens close to the house, but in proportion to the park, they have been on a relatively small scale. The family's main interest, so far as parks and gardens were concerned, lay in Hurstbourne Park and Eggesford, until the 9th Earl took Farleigh in hand.

In the 1990s, Lady Portsmouth and her designer Georgia Langton began work on redesigning the grounds. After the relics of the school buildings had been cleared, there was a blank canvas on which to create a modern version of the former pleasure grounds, with woodland walks, water features, formal and informal gardens, glasshouses and a lake. Farleigh now plays host to concerts, cricket matches, carriage-driving and even an annual raft race. If Sir Henry Wallop were to return with Elizabeth and her court, he would quickly feel at home.

The park gates leading to the lake

St Andrew's Church, Farleigh Wallop

EPILOGUE

The Wallop family already had a distinguished history before Sir Henry, but rose even further, with the grant of the earldom in the eighteenth century. Since then the title has passed to a variety of characters, some colourful, some influential. Estates have altered, homes have come and gone, but farming and gardening have been constant themes. Farleigh House has been rebuilt, enlarged and restored. Now, in the twenty-first century, Sir Henry's descendants can look back on a thousand years with pride, and forward with confidence.

A view of the garden at Farleigh House

REFERENCES

ABBREVIATIONS

HRO: Hampshire Record Office
PRO: Public Record Office, now The National Archives
WSRO: West Suffolk Record Office

1 V. J. Watney, *The Wallop Family and their Ancestry* (4 vols., Oxford, 1928). The early history of the family is derived from his work.

2 Watney, *Wallop Family*, 1, xxvii.

3 *Oxford Dictionary of National Biography*, (60 vols., Oxford, 2004), 57, 29–33.

4 W. J. Ferrar, *Songs of Wallop* (Winchester, 1936), no. 3.

5 Watney, *Wallop Family*, 1, xxviii.

6 Watney, *Wallop Family*, 1, xxxv.

7 *ODNB*, 57, 27–9.

8 R. H. Fritze, 'The role of family and religion in the local politics of early Elizabethan England: the case of Hampshire in the 1560's', *Historical Journal*, 25 (1982), 267–87.

9 Q. G. C. Wallop, 10th Earl of Portsmouth, *Farleigh House: a History* (typescript, 2003).

10 J. Stevenson, ed. *Correspondence of Sir Henry Unton* (London, 1847), nos. 42–3.

11 E. K. Chambers, *The Elizabethan Stage* (4 vols. Oxford, 1923), 1, 123–4.

12 J. Osborne, *Entertaining Elizabeth I: the Progresses and Great Houses of her Time* (London, 1989), 88–92; A. Weir, *Elizabeth the Queen* (London, 1998), 262–8.

13 D. J. H. Clifford, ed. *The Diaries of Lady Anne Clifford* (Stroud, 1992), 26.

14 Watney, *Wallop Family*, 1, xlvi–iii.

15 *ODNB*, 57, 35–6.

16 Watney, *Wallop Family*, 1, xlix.

17 Watney, *Wallop Family*, 1, liii; website: www.familysearch.org

18 Watney, *Wallop Family*, 1, liii.

19 Watney, *Wallop Family*, 1, liv.

20 Portsmouth, *Farleigh House*.

21 HRO 44M69/F3/6/19: copy of inventory of Dorothy Wallop, 1704.

22 Watney, *Wallop Family*, 1, lv–vi.

23 *ODNB*, 57, 34–5.

24 A. M. Deveson, 'Hurstbourne Park: image and reality', *Hampshire Studies*, 59 (2004), 198–200.

25 *Victoria County History of Hampshire* (5 vols., London, 1905–14), iv, 611.

26 Deveson, 'Hurstbourne Park', 201.

27   C. Hussey, 'Farleigh House, Hampshire', *Country Life* (1941), 479.

28   HRO 15M84/5/3/1/1: letters of Newton Fellowes, 4th Earl of Portsmouth.

29   *A Genuine Report of the Proceedings on the Portsmouth Case* (London, 1823), 7.

30   W. and R. A. Austen-Leigh, *Jane Austen: her Life and Letters*, 2nd ed. (London, 1913), 150–1.

31   C. Tomalin, *Jane Austen: a Life* (London, 1997), 88–9.

32   HRO 15M84/5/4/14: letter from Mrs Alder to the 5th Earl of Portsmouth, 1859.

33   Watney, *Wallop Family*, 1, lxvii.

34   HRO 15M84/F25: notebook of Newton Wallop, 6th Earl of Portsmouth, c. 1892.

35   L. Edel, *Henry James: the Conquest of London, 1870-1883* (London, 1962), 362–3.

36   Watney, *Wallop Family*, 1, lxix.

37   HRO 15M84/5/7/5: correspondence relating to offer of Garter, 1869.

38   HRO 15M84/5/9/3/9: newspaper cutting, 1892.

39   A. M. Deveson, 'The lost mansions of Hurstbourne Park', *Hampshire Field Club and Archaeological Society Newsletter*, 43 (2005), 33–5.

40   HRO 15M84/4/24: Guisachan visitors' book, 1905–31.

41   Watney, *Wallop Family*, 1, lxxi.

42   S. Morton, *Where the Rivers Run North* (Sheridan, Wyoming, 2007).

43   *ODNB*, 57, 26–7; G. V. Wallop, 9th Earl of Portsmouth, *A Knot of Roots: an Autobiography* (London, 1965), chs. 1–2.

44   HRO 15M84/5/14/27: scrapbook, nineteenth–twentieth centuries.

45   *ODNB*, 57, 27.

46   Watney, *Wallop Family*, 1, lvii–lviii.

47   Watney, *Wallop Family*, 1, Appendix iv.

48   HRO 15M84/F25.

49   HRO 15M84/F27: notebook of Beatrice, Countess of Portsmouth, 1901-05.

50   Watney, *Wallop Family*, 1, lxvii; HRO 15M84/F27.

51   Watney, *Wallop Family*, 1, lxvii.

52   HRO 15M84/F27.

53   HRO 15M84/5/6/2 and 5: notebooks of Lady Catherine Fellowes, nineteenth century.

54   HRO 15M84/F27.

55   HRO 15M84/5/4/11: correspondence of the 3rd Earl of Portsmouth, nineteenth century.

56   Watney, *Wallop Family*, 1, lxviii.

57   W. Gardner, Lady Burghclere, *Eveline, Countess of Portsmouth: a Recollection by her Niece* (priv. publ., London, 1907).

58   HRO 15M84/5/8/4/12: record book of Eveline, Countess of Portsmouth, nineteenth century.

59   F. E. Hardy, *The Early Life of Thomas Hardy, 1840-1891* (London, 1928), 221–3.

60   Deveson, 'Hurstbourne Park', 200–204.

61   WSRO E2/33/2: Sir John Cullum's tour of the West Country, 1779; HRO 15M84/P3/284: engraving of Hurstbourne Park, 1783.

62   *Hampshire Directory* (1792), 937–8.

63 H. M. Colvin, *Biographical Dictionary of British Architects, 1600-1840*, 3rd ed. (London, 1995), 649.

64 HRO 15M84/5/10/1/2: diary of Beatrice, Countess of Portsmouth, 1891-5.

65 HRO TOP/173/2/5: J. Netherclift, Plan of an estate [Hurstbourne], 1817.

66 Farleigh Estate Office, photograph of Hurstbourne Park.

67 HRO 15M84/5/10/1/2.

68 *Hampshire Chronicle*, December 8, 1917.

69 HRO 15M84/5/9/2/11: correspondence, 1897.

70 HRO 15M84/6/4: photograph album, c. 1897.

71 Farleigh Estate Office, plans by J. Mackie Murray, 1936; plans by Beeston, Burmester and Galsworthy for additions to the kitchen wing in 1907.

72 *Shell Guide to Ireland,* 2nd ed. (London, 1967), 273; HRO 15M84/6/4: loose photograph of Enniscorthy Castle, 1895.

73 HRO 15M84/3/2/4/3: papers relating to purchase of Guisachan, 1905.

74 HRO 15M84/3/2/5/1: notebook and notes, 1905-15.

75 HRO 15M84/4/24: Guisachan visitors' book, 1905-31.

76 D. Fraser, *Guisachan: a History*, 2nd ed. (priv. publ., 1998), 31.

77 Watney, *Wallop Family*, 1, ii, 309.

78 HRO 15M84/F27.

79 Worsley, G. 'Farleigh House, Hampshire', *Country Life* (1994), 64.

80 *VCH*, iv, 532.

81 *VCH*, iii, 365.

82 PRO PROB11/95: will of Sir Henry Wallop, 1599.

83 Edward Roberts, personal communication.

84 *VCH,* iii, 365.

85 E. Hughes and P. White, eds. *The Hampshire Hearth Tax Assessment*, 1665 (Winchester, 1991), 218.

86 Portsmouth, *Farleigh House*; Michael Bullen, personal communication.

87 PRO PROB4/2942: inventory of Henry Wallop, 1691.

88 HRO 44M69/F3/6/19.

89 Hussey, 'Farleigh House, Hampshire', 476; Worsley, 'Farleigh House, Hampshire', 62.

90 HRO 15M84/3/1/1/94: lease of Farleigh House to Peter Serle, previous tenant Morgan Deane, 1737.

91 Farleigh Estate Office, estate plan, 1745; HRO 15M84/MP10: estate plan, 1787.

92 HRO 15M84/3/1/3/5: correspondence 1894-1905; 15M84/3/1/1/104, 108-9, 692: leases of Farleigh House, nineteenth-twentieth centuries.

93 The Hon. Nicholas Wallop and Lady Jane Wallop, personal communications.

BIBLIOGRAPHY

UNPUBLISHED SOURCES

THE NATIONAL ARCHIVES

PROB 4/2942: inventory of Henry Wallop, 1691.
PROB 11/95: will of Sir Henry Wallop, 1599.

HAMPSHIRE RECORD OFFICE

44M69/F3/6/19: copy of inventory of Dorothy Wallop, 1704.
15M84: Wallop papers.
TOP/173/2/5: J. Netherclift, Plan of an estate [Hurstbourne Park], 1817.

WEST SUFFOLK RECORD OFFICE

E2/33/2: Sir John Cullum's Tour of the West Country, 1779.

FARLEIGH ESTATE OFFICE

Wallop, Q. G. C., 10th Earl of Portsmouth, *Farleigh House: a History* (typescript, 2003).
Photograph of Hurstbourne Park in the late-nineteenth century.
Plan of Farleigh Estate, 1745.
Plans of Hurstbourne Park, 1907 and 1936.

PUBLISHED SOURCES

Austen-Leigh, W. and R. A. *Jane Austen: her Life and Letters*, 2nd ed. (London, 1913).
Chambers, E. K. *The Elizabethan Stage* (4 vols., Oxford, 1923).
Clifford, D. J. H., ed. *The Diaries of Lady Anne Clifford* (Stroud, 1992).
Colvin, H. M. *Biographical Dictionary of British Architects*, 1600-1840, 3rd ed. (London, 1995).
Deveson, A. M. 'Hurstbourne Park: image and reality', *Hampshire Studies*, 59 (2004), 196-209.
Deveson, A. M. 'The lost mansions of Hurstbourne Park', *Hampshire Field Club and Archaeological Society Newsletter,* 43 (2005), 31-6.
Edel, L. *Henry James: the Conquest of London*, 1870-1883 (London, 1962).
Ferrar, W. J. *Songs of Wallop* (Winchester, 1936).
Fraser, D. *Guisachan: a History*, 2nd ed. (priv. publ., 1998).
Fritze, R. H. 'The role of family and religion in the local politics of early Elizabethan England: the case of Hampshire in the 1560s', *Historical Journal,* 25 (1982), 267-87.
Gardner, W., Lady Burghclere *Eveline, Countess of Portsmouth: a Recollection by her Niece* (priv. publ., London, 1907).
A Genuine Report of the Proceedings on the Portsmouth Case (London, 1823).
Hampshire Chronicle, December 8, 1917.
Hampshire Directory (1792).

Hardy, F. E. *The Early Life of Thomas Hardy*, 1840-1891 (London, 1928).

Hughes, E. and White, P., eds. *The Hampshire Hearth Tax Assessment*, 1665 (Winchester, 1991).

Hussey, C. 'Farleigh House, Hampshire', *Country Life* (1941), 476-9, 536-9.

Morton, S. *Where the Rivers Run North* (Sheridan, Wyoming, 2007).

Osborne, J. *Entertaining Elizabeth I: the Progresses and Great Houses of her Time* (London, 1989).

Oxford Dictionary of National Biography (60 vols., Oxford, 2004).

Shell Guide to Ireland, 2nd ed. (London, 1967).

Stevenson, J., ed. *Correspondence of Sir Henry Unton* (London, 1847).

Tomalin, C. *Jane Austen: a Life* (London, 1997).

Victoria County History of Hampshire (5 vols., London, 1903–14).

Wallop, G.V., 9th Earl of Portsmouth, *A Knot of Roots: an Autobiography* (London, 1965).

Watney, V. J. *The Wallop Family and their Ancestry* (4 vols., Oxford, 1928).

Weir, A. *Elizabeth the Queen* (London, 1998).

Worsley, G. 'Farleigh House, Hampshire', *Country Life* (1994), 62-5.

WEBSITE

www.familysearch.org

A mermaid at the entrance gates to Farleigh House

A mermaid holding up a comb and looking glass is the crest on the Wallop coat of arms. The arms are Argent, a bend wavy sable, the supporters are two chamois or wild goats sable and the motto is En Suivant La Vérité.

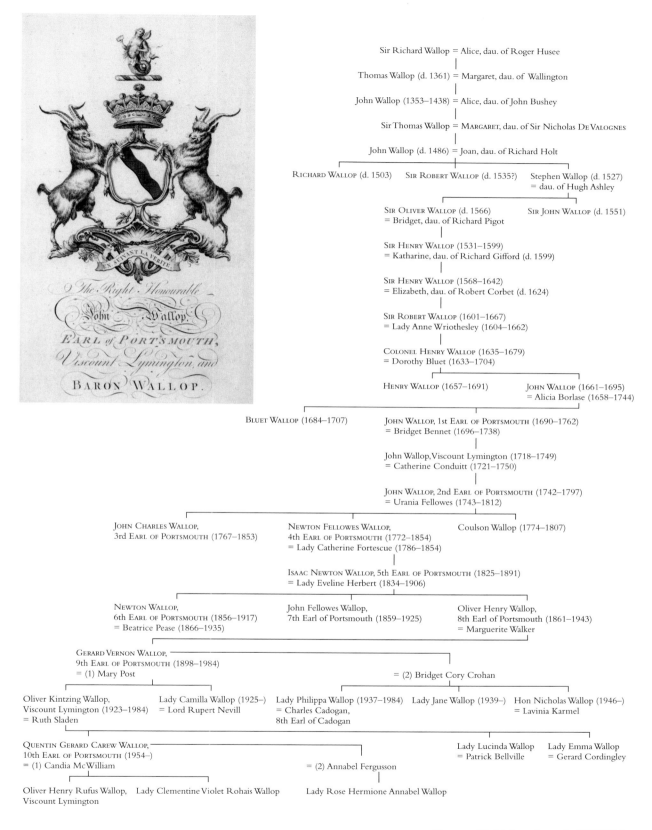

The Right Honourable
John Wallop,
EARL of PORTSMOUTH,
Viscount Lymington, and
BARON WALLOP.

EN SUIVANT LA VERITÉ.

Sir Richard Wallop = Alice, dau. of Roger Husee

Thomas Wallop (d. 1361) = Margaret, dau. of Wallington

John Wallop (1353–1438) = Alice, dau. of John Bushey

Sir Thomas Wallop = MARGARET, dau. of Sir Nicholas DE VALOGNES

John Wallop (d. 1486) = Joan, dau. of Richard Holt

RICHARD WALLOP (d. 1503)   SIR ROBERT WALLOP (d. 1535?)   Stephen Wallop (d. 1527)
= dau. of Hugh Ashley

SIR OLIVER WALLOP (d. 1566)   SIR JOHN WALLOP (d. 1551)
= Bridget, dau. of Richard Pigot

SIR HENRY WALLOP (1531–1599)
= Katharine, dau. of Richard Gifford (d. 1599)

SIR HENRY WALLOP (1568–1642)
= Elizabeth, dau. of Robert Corbet (d. 1624)

SIR ROBERT WALLOP (1601–1667)
= Lady Anne Wriothesley (1604–1662)

COLONEL HENRY WALLOP (1635–1679)
= Dorothy Bluet (1633–1704)

HENRY WALLOP (1657–1691)   JOHN WALLOP (1661–1695)
= Alicia Borlase (1658–1744)

BLUET WALLOP (1684–1707)   JOHN WALLOP, 1st EARL OF PORTSMOUTH (1690–1762)
= Bridget Bennet (1696–1738)

John Wallop, Viscount Lymington (1718–1749)
= Catherine Conduitt (1721–1750)

JOHN WALLOP, 2nd EARL OF PORTSMOUTH (1742–1797)
= Urania Fellowes (1743–1812)

JOHN CHARLES WALLOP,   NEWTON FELLOWES WALLOP,   Coulson Wallop (1774–1807)
3rd EARL OF PORTSMOUTH (1767–1853)   4th EARL OF PORTSMOUTH (1772–1854)
= Lady Catherine Fortescue (1786–1854)

ISAAC NEWTON WALLOP, 5th EARL OF PORTSMOUTH (1825–1891)
= Lady Eveline Herbert (1834–1906)

NEWTON WALLOP,   John Fellowes Wallop,   Oliver Henry Wallop,
6th EARL OF PORTSMOUTH (1856–1917)   7th Earl of Portsmouth (1859–1925)   8th Earl of Portsmouth (1861–1943)
= Beatrice Pease (1866–1935)   = Marguerite Walker

GERARD VERNON WALLOP,
9th EARL OF PORTSMOUTH (1898–1984)
= (1) Mary Post   = (2) Bridget Cory Crohan

Oliver Kintzing Wallop,   Lady Camilla Wallop (1925–)   Lady Philippa Wallop (1937–1984)   Lady Jane Wallop (1939–)   Hon Nicholas Wallop (1946–)
Viscount Lymington (1923–1984)   = Lord Rupert Nevill   = Charles Cadogan,   = Lavinia Karmel
= Ruth Sladen   8th Earl of Cadogan

QUENTIN GERARD CAREW WALLOP,   Lady Lucinda Wallop   Lady Emma Wallop
10th EARL OF PORTSMOUTH (1954–)   = Patrick Bellville   = Gerard Cordingley
= (1) Candia McWilliam   = (2) Annabel Fergusson

Oliver Henry Rufus Wallop,   Lady Clementine Violet Rohais Wallop   Lady Rose Hermione Annabel Wallop
Viscount Lymington

Owners of Farleigh are shown in CAPITALS